When a person completes 90 years of age without a single day of hospitalization, without any surgical intervention in his body and no age related issues, the ingredients of living and thinking that he has adopted & applied, ought to be shared with people. Hence this book.

According to the author, the secrets of good health of his father, Prof. B. N. Chaulkar is his thought processes, which he calls as "Internal Operating Procedures." The life of Prof. Chaulkar is a validation of the axiom

"You reap in what you sow"

The principles of goodness, honesty and integrity that he has followed throughout his life is visible in the harmony and good health that he is maintaining in his nineties. The book reveals the values, beliefs and ethics required for a fulfilling and purposeful life.

An inspiration for people of all ages.

Father@90

First Impression 2022

Initiated by :
Prabha Guidance and Life Coaching
B/2, Sweta Park Society,
Tulsidham – GIDC Road,
Manjalpur,
Vadodara – 390011
Email – prabha.guidance_lifecoaching@yahoo.com
Mobile No. 9825917518

Designed by :
Jayshree Printery
15/16, Laxmi Estate, 1st Floor,
Bahucharaji Mandir Road, Karelibaug,
Vadodara - 390018, Gujarat, India.
M : 94280 67484

This book is dedicated to our

Mother

Mrs. Prabhavati Bhalchandra Chaulkar

*Her life partnership of 62 years with father
has been fundamental to his persona*

Contents

Acknowledgments

I would like to express my profound gratitude to the legacy of His Highness Maharaja Sayajirao Gaekwad III, Founder of M. S. University, an educational institute and Bank of Baroda, a financial enterprise. Father served in M. S. University for 34 years and I served in Bank of Baroda for 36 years. So, we have been blessed by the wisdom of Maharaja Sayajirao Gaekwad III, collectively for 70 years, 9 of those years overlapping. Maharaja's vision has enabled countless Indians in finding true and fulfilling vocation.

I would like to express my gratitude to Dr. Arvind Vartak, "Bhai" as we affectionately call him, for writing the Forward to this book. He and father have shared their childhood and his insights helped me in adding lustre to this opus.

I would like to thank Prof. (Dr) Anjali Karolia, Dean, Faculty of Family and Community Sciences, M. S. University of Baroda and Prof.(Dr) Madhu Sharan, Head and Associate Director, Department of Clothing & Textiles, Faculty of Family and Community Sciences, M. S. University of Baroda for giving the students' perspective and expressing deep regards for the esteemed contribution of father in their lives.

Thanks are due to Hema Vahini, Mamata, Satish Bhauji,

Nishit, Sushama Vahini, Minal, Shishir and their children for being on the stage and playing their part.

I would like to express my gratitude to Mandu Tai, Ajit Bhauji, Pushpa, Arvind Bhauji, Pravin, Anila Vahini, Amita and Milind and their children for the sharing the life space and making life exciting.

Thanks are due to all my Uncles and Aunty's on my mother's side and their children, their spouses for adding lustre to the relationships.

A special thank you to all our neighbours in Jai Ratna Building for being available for each other in happy and sad times. The ingredients of community living, which we experienced and enjoyed at Jai Ratna, will always be cherished by us. The major values of living harmoniously were imbibed over there.

I would like to express my gratitude to the thirteen Ph.D students of father. Father never boasted that he had guided so many Ph.D students. He always maintained that he could be guide because there were students willing to learn from him. Similarly thanks are due to a multitude of other students who were fortunate enough to be his students.

I would like to pay homage to the memory of Prof. R. L. Desai, who was instrumental in bringing father to Baroda and Prof. Miss. Justina Singh, who was Guru for father.

I would like to pay homage to our Grand Parents, father's parents as well as mother's parents, for their influence which equipped him with great wisdom to live confidently.

I would also like to pay homage to Tai, Bhau, Aaka, Dada and all of his brother-in-laws, sister-in-laws who have passed over, but have left a lasting impression on him.

Homage is due to Aanna (Karulkar), Mane Kaka, Pappa (M.S. Sawant) Aaka, Aapa (Falnikar), Tatya & Kaku (Marathe), Nargolwala Maushi, Kale Kaka and Kaki, Bhabha and Amma (Amlani), Warty Kaka & Kaki who were amongst the elders in Jai Ratna.

Last, but not the least, I am thankful to my wife, Bhavana and daughter, Prachiti for patiently observing my effort and then doing the first editing of this work.

Vadodara

10th November 2022					Nilesh B. Chaulkar

Forward

Dr. Bhalchandra Narayan Chaulkar is my Mama (Maternal Uncle). I am glad that I was associated with this very unusual joint family. Family consisted of different family names RANEs, CHAULKARs, VARTAKs, MEKDEs. It will be impossible to describe this family without the mention of Mrs. Tarabai Rane. She was the undeclared head of family as the eldest sister in Chaulkar family. Her husband Mr. Harishchandra Rane who was a great supporter to everyone without any expectation of any return. I had a great pleasure of being with my Mama. He is eleven years elder to me. However, it was my great pleasure to be vehemently arguing with him on any subject on this earth. The matters extended from local social issues to anything like international politics or may be newer scientific developments. On most of the occasions I was a looser in the discussions.

Dr. Bhalchandra Chaulkar is a very simple person and totally unassuming. The manner in which he always carried himself never ever expressed the level of his intelligence nor he showed off his education at high level of BSc, BSc(Tech) and PhD from Wisconsin University in USA. I strongly feel like telling my experience after he returned from USA. We were travelling from Mumbai to Saaral, his native family house. At that time, a thought came to my mind that this gentleman has just returned about five days back from USA. However, it never appeared in his style that one would doubt if he ever had been abroad.

I was extremely fortunate in getting suitable guidance from him all the time. The guidance I received on various matters relating to family or otherwise, has always proved to be correct. On educational front, I was getting great support on unfortunate occasions like failures and also in choosing the medical career in particular. There was no match ever to his suggestions in every aspect. On every occasion, however small, it may be I followed his advice, even though I did not agree with him. On most of the occasions, his guidance has been proved beneficial to me.

Because of the distance, diminished hearing and with advancing age of both of us, the occasions for arguments have now been reduced. I will never forget enjoying the pleasure of disagreements with each other.

He has now crossed Ninety. I am glad that he is still without any significant illness and enjoying good health. This is all on account of a very simple lifestyle and tremendous control on his diet.

I sincerely wish him long and healthy years ahead.

I have gone through the manuscript of this biography. It is written by my cousin, his youngest son Nilesh. He has done a remarkable job. Such work requires lot of efforts. Nilesh has taken a lot of pains in gathering the information and presenting the same in this book. I know that he has been doing this work over a long period of time. It needs authentication too.

I am sure that the readers, particularly his students and acquaintances, will find it interesting and will enjoy the nostalgia of the memories of the yesteryears.

Mumbai

21st June, 2022.   Dr. Arvind Vartak

A tribute to my Mentor and Guru
Prof. B. N. Chaulkar

As a young girl of nineteen I decided to come to The Maharaja Sayajirao University of Baroda to pursue my Master in Clothing and Textiles after completing my Under Graduation from Punjab Agriculture University Ludhiana. On arrival here to Baroda and my entry into the department we were greeted by our Head of the Department Prof B. N. Chaulkar. He would take most of our courses in Textiles – Chemistry, Testing, Colour and Finishing and also all courses in Research methodology, so in short most subjects were taught by him. I still remember the first few classes all of us classmates would be looking at each other and wondered what is it that he was wanting us to understand! We were given the references and were expected to read up every day and make our own notes. It is only when we finally started doing our self-study and putting our notes together that we understood what he was wanting us to know. He was so rich in knowledge and his concepts so clear that we used to be in awe of him. He knew Booth and Trotman textbooks cover to cover. His application of this knowledge to research was amazing and he would put it so simply that we never realized when he started making us think of more complex problems. He was a great scholar who passionately shared what he had learned in many years of experience. I stand here today to attest that the person I have become today has been greatly influenced by his teachings.

Sir was a man of very high principles. His simplicity, his quiet way of telling you what he appreciated and what he did not. His calm disposition said a lot and as students we were well aware of what he approved and what he did not in spite of him never saying or being strict with us.

He was my mentor for my Masters dissertation and I still remember when I had to give my defense for my research the tips that he gave me - that I know my work the best and so be confident and lead the examiners to the questions you want them to ask. Till today after 40 years of being in the profession I still tell my students the same thing while they are preparing for their examination and I remember him so fondly.

He was instrumental in getting me to this department to teach. During my student days I would tell him that I want to be a professor in a college and to my surprise the day I completed my masters and after two or three days I was called from the hostel by him to the department and he asked me to go into a first year class and engage them. I still remember how nervous I was and asked him how am I going to do that, his answer was simple you said you wanted to be a teacher now I am giving you the opportunity to do so! That is how my career started! I owe my entire 40 years of teaching career to him. His guidance right through my early years. His insistence and guidance for registering for Ph.D. I will always be indebted to him for it. He knew what was good for us and his subtle comments push in the right direction, has always been a blessing for me.

My parents also had very high regard for him and would always make it a point to meet him and ask about me and would be satisfied that I had a mentor who cared for his students. Sir's small gestures of being with our family for my engagement, letters with wishes for our daughter when she was born, and his condolence messages on the demise of my parents have always meant a lot to me.

I still remember his words when I took charge as the Dean of the faculty and I went to meet him and take his blessing. His first statement to me was "Have you read the University Handbook?" Now that you are sitting on this chair you must be very sure of all the rules and don't ever sign anywhere blindly!

I have never forgotten his advice, his values that he has inculcated in me as a teacher, administrator and a colleague and always hope and pray that he would be proud of me and I don't let him down.

It is he who has shown me what it is like to be a great teacher. It is from him that I understood that a teacher needs to be supportive, understanding, and have a passion for what they are doing. It is he who has truly inspired me.

So, I just want to say thank you for being a wonderful role model for me. I have achieved the most of my career goal by constantly following all the advice and tips from him. I am so grateful for the opportunity to pen my thoughts about my association with him.

Thank you,

Prof. Anjali Karolia
Dean
Faculty of Family and Community Sciences
The Maharaja Sayajirao University of Baroda

Vadodara

21st August, 2022.

Memoirs of an educator

Humble, visionary, non-egoistical, inventive, self-sufficient, motivational...

Can you think of any person with all above qualities? It's none other than Dr. B.N. Chaulkar, or "Chaulkar Sir" as we all call him. I feel privileged for having the opportunity to study under him for all of my higher education, including my Ph.D. It is indeed, very difficult to express my gratitude to him in a page or two.

Sir is a visionary in the real sense. As a student, I never realized how well-planned sir's administrative activities were. But now, as an educator myself, I can see how meticulous was Sir's road map for the development of the department was. He built the Department from scratch and inspired future leaders to develop it even further. The result of such a powerful foundation is in the form of the well-established Department of Clothing and Textiles today running four UG programs, two PG programs and Ph.D. program. The inventive, ingenious nature of his boosted quality teaching and inspired students to become stellar learners.

A simple, humble personality holding a gold mine of intellect, he has been a teacher in real sense. Even now, he provides me with guidance, be it in the field of teaching or even administration. His unique approach to problem-solving is commendable, regardless of the field. Be it language barriers, student submissions, research guidance...no obstacle is too big for him to overcome.

A self-sufficient personality, who never abused his

power or authority. He is, and never was, a people pleaser and did what he felt was right. His blessings, guidance and teachings have helped hundreds of students who are now holding prestigious positions at different platforms other than academics as well.

His vision, guidance, encouragement, motivation, problem-solving approach and encouraging healthy discussions are the traits which have influenced me a lot. I am fortunate that he has been there for all my important professional milestones. In 1986, he was my teacher at the degree program. In 1988, he was my guide for dissertation. In 1998, he used to come as a visiting professor at S. P. University, V. V. Nagar where I started my career as lecturer. In 2000, I enrolled as a Ph.D. student under him. And most recently, in 2021, I had the privilege and honor to celebrate his birthday in the Department as the Head of the Department.

A teacher is always a teacher, and this reflects in Sir's personality. Even today, you can turn to him for genuine guidance and constructive criticism. He is a real gem of a person. I pray for his healthy life and hope to have his guidance for many more years to come.

Prof. Madhu Sharan
Head & Associate Director
Department of Clothing and Textiles
Faculty of Family and Community Sciences
The Maharaja Sayajirao University of Baroda

Vadodara
5th July, 2022.

Introduction

On 18th October, 2021 father completed 90 years of age. A tremendous milestone. He is a man who does not like a show of emotions, whether joyful or sad and so we celebrated the occasion with presentation of an album having around 155 pictures depicting his journey from his young days till Ganesh Utsav at home in September, 2021. On 19thOctober, 2021 his students invited him at the Department of Clothing and Textiles, at the erstwhile Faculty of Home Science, now Faculty of Family & Community Sciences, for a brief celebrations with ex-staff and students.

There was a brief birthday party for him – a cake cutting ceremony, some snacks and chatting over in the meeting. During that talk he was asked the secret of his good health. And he told them that he regularly goes for a walk – 20 minutes in the morning and 20 minutes in the evening. Besides he does some brisk jumping exercise for around 10 minutes. (Just jumping on his toes and not raising the body too high)

Whatever mentioned above is true. But that is not the only secret of his good health. The secret is his attitude towards life – his thinking, his beliefs, right from the beginning – as far as I have seen him since my childhood and what mother used to tell us about their early days. I will share my learning's from his life since I have had the privilege of observing him from very close quarters.

One of the most incredible aspects of his journey has been the fact that in 90 years of his life, he has never been hospitalised for any illness or injury and there has been no surgical intervention in his body, except for removal of an odd tooth here and there. He says that he was born in a farm, outside the village, in a makeshift home, since the village was in the grip of the epidemic of plague. So his birth was also not in any hospital as the case is in today's times.

As I was reviewing and editing the contents of the book, father turned 91 on 18th October, 2022. It has been a tremendous year full of learning. He revealed that he does not allow the pains and aches of the body to affect his mind. So the pain is there, but suffering is optional. Besides, he has been an embodiment of abundance. His life reveals that abundance is a mind set. In the year bygone, war in Ukraine has been a dampener. For a person who had been around when World War II took place, the sufferings of the people affected by war pains him.

I have narrated some of our stories, which reveal his values, beliefs and approach to life. Some valuable lessons for living are disclosed in the stories. I desire that the readers dwell-on them. It will help them enormously in handling twists and turns on the road called LIFE.

1.   He has been a strict vegetarian.

It is very difficult to maintain your perspective of eating habits, in a family where non vegetarian food is the staple diet. In my early days, I could not understand how he remained a strict vegetarian where consumption of non vegetarian food – chicken, mutton, fish, prawn, etc was extensive. Everyone cherished those foodies, but father was never affected by their choice. Mother used to tell, that previously he used to have eggs – omelette and boiled eggs for breakfast. But I have never seen him having omelette and eggs. When we were young, we were not allowed to bring chicken or mutton at home. He never disallowed us from eating non vegetarian food, but chicken and mutton were not cooked in our home during our childhood. (He relaxed that rule in the year 1981, when my sister Mamata, along with her husband Satish, our cousin sister Pushpa and her husband Arvind visited us.)   But he never had a desire to eat non vegetarian food of any sort.

According to me, being a strict vegetarian has been one of the most significant reasons for maintaining good health. Now a days, lot of debates are being held in general and on social media on the benefits of being a vegan and people are shifting their preferences for the being a complete vegetarian person. Our digestive system is not made for consumption of meat and flesh and so consumption of such food adds toxicity, which results in damage to the mechanism of the bodily system. Father's preference for only vegetarian diet has prevented invasion of toxicity to his body. "This is my belief."

2. He has been a teetotaler throughout his life.

This habit goes along side the first habit of being a vegetarian person. He spent 3 years of his young days in Madison, Wisconsin State, USA pursing his doctorial studies. It was extremely cold during the winters and anybody would be convinced to have a warm dose of brandy or whisky in the chilly and snowy weather. But he was never drawn towards this habit. He has never touched alcohol in his life. Same about smoking. He has never touched a cigarette.

Now a days, we hear a lot about the harmful effects of alcohol and smoking. He avoided these things right from the beginning, knowing fully well the ill effects it can have on the body.

3. He has been an extremely honest person. Very ethical.

I have never seen my father being dishonest with anyone or in any situation. He has been an embodiment of truth and honesty. This one struck me quite early in my life. Ours was a Mumbai based family (in our childhood). During school days, we used to travel to Mumbai and then to Alibag during vacations in Summer and Diwali. When we completed 12 years of age, he started purchasing full tickets for us – railways and bus journeys. Many of his contemporaries would advise him to keep purchasing half tickets – no one checks the age of children. (During those days we were not supposed to carry any identification proof). But truthfulness has been his hallmark. At that time, he was the only person earning in the family and there were a total of six persons dependant on him. We - four siblings, mother and our aunty Tai. His honesty paid him tremendously when in the last 7 to 8 years of his job, we were all earning members and mother was the only person who was not a wage earner in the family. I can tell about many such examples, wherein he has refused to succumb to the dictates of dishonesty. This attitude has helped him handle many uncomfortable moments with higher authorities – whether in the Faculty, University or Society.

4. Gratefulness has been his distinguishing characteristic.

He has never forgotten the role played by his elder sister - Tai and brother-in-law, Bhau, in his life. He used to tell us – if Tai and Bhau had not been there to take care of us, we would not have been able to chart this route in our lives. [Father rose to the level of Professor and my Uncle was General Manager in Shipping Corporation of India]

He has never forgotten the contribution of Prof. R. L. Desai and Prof. Miss. Justina Singh in his career. Once when I asked him how he came to know about the vacancy in Baroda University. He told me that Prof. Desai had come to Mumbai and he told him that since he was qualified for the post of lecturer, he should apply for the same. At that time, there was an uproar in the corridors of the faculty as he was an outsider. The other two candidates, however, were not adequately qualified for the post. Those two gentlemen then became close friends of father and I remember been at their homes. Our families bonded quite well. I remembered how revered Prof. Desai was for him. He used to come to our Jai Ratna building residence and he would call father from the ground arena and father would immediately go and meet him downstairs. Same with Prof. Justina Singh. I can recollect her visit to our place. The day she passed away, father looked very sad. I asked mother why father's mood is gloomy. She replied, Miss. Singh passed away.

Even today, he gratefully remembers Tai, Aaka, Bhau, Prof. Desai and Prof. Miss. Justina Singh. He has also found memories of his younger brother-in-law, Mr. Madhusudan Vartak, father of Dr. Arvind Vartak. He told me that he was a very helpful person. One of his friend's was infected with TB and Mr. Madhusudan Vartak would go and take care of him. As a result, he unfortunately got infected with TB and then passed away. And the irony is that the person who was initially infected with TB got well and survived. The incident, a catastrophic moment at that time, possibly, imbibed values of sacrifice for the benefit and well-being of others.

Being grateful is a part of his being. He has this habit of saying –thank you- even for a small gesture of collecting any item. For example saying thank you to the sales person after purchase of goods, to the fruit vendor after purchasing fruits. Thus saying thank you, being grateful is imbibed in him. Now a days, we come across so many therapies, wherein we are advised to "Be happy and give thanks." Father has not attended any therapy. He has a built in mechanism of gratefulness.

5. He never displayed ego of his high qualifications and his position.

This one was evident in his correspondence with our school authorities, while acknowledging the report cards, leave applications, etc. The letter was never signed as Dr. B. N. Chaulkar. Only B. N. Chaulkar. He never displayed his credentials where they were not required. People in our neighbourhood knew about his stature, but in the interaction with neighbours he has always been a friendly and sociable person

Once a foreign student, from Africa came to our house searching for father. At that time, he was the in-charge Dean. She came in an auto rickshaw and after stepping down from the auto, she asked the shop keepers on the ground floor of the building. "Where is Dr. Chaulkar staying?" A young lady, who knew us, only heard word 'doctor' and replied – There is no doctor staying in this building. The student from Africa continued her search in the auto for about an hour in the vicinity and again came back to Jai Ratna Building. At that time, she specifically stressed the surname. She was then escorted to our home.

The people around never got an inkling about his stature in professional life. He followed simple living and never displayed an iota of pride. His simplicity caught with us as well. He had an account with Bank of Baroda, University Campus Branch. One of my friends was posted at that branch and one day, he asked me who is Prof. Chaulkar. When I told him, he is my father, he was also surprised. He replied, but Prof. Chaulkar stays in the University Campus. I had to reply, "No we stay at Jai Ratna Building."

6. He has never harbored any grudges or resentments towards anyone.

Father used to have his own point of view, which he hardly compromised. He used to place his point very emphatically.   Sometimes he would get upset by the other person's thinking. But he was gracious enough to accept the contrary view. In the discussions, though he was emphatic, he never suggested that he was correct. After the discussions were over, he would forget the episode. I have not seen him label any one for his or her view or behavior.   He has a saying – If they don't understand what can I do and leave the matter over there.

Similarly, he would be pained to see someone being unauthentic or unethical in the family. But he never branded that person. He used to remark, possibly that person has not evolved properly.

7. He has never displayed any craving or attachment towards money.

This will surprise people. Yes, but I have never seen any person being so averse to money. When he retired from service in the year 1991, the University authorities, did not pay him the gratuity amount of Rs. 75,000/-. He has always been a "Swabhimani" person and refused to go the University office and plead for his dues. He believed that he had completed all the procedural work and it was the duty of the concerned persons to pay the amount with due respect.   But no communication was forthcoming from the University office and he also seemed to be uninterested in the same. One day, my friend, who happens to be a faculty member in University came home and he was told that father has not yet received the gratuity amount. He assured me that he will inquire and convey what is the issue. A few days later he came home and told me that the cheque is ready and the authorities only require his signature on the acknowledgement. He suggested that father just put his signature on the revenue stamp and he will manage to bring the gratuity cheque. So father agreed to put his signature on the revenue stamp and handed it to him.   In a couple of days, he brought home the gratuity cheque of Rs.75000/-,which was dated a few days after his retirement day in the year 1991.   The cheque was revalidated and a new date stamp was put on the same and authenticated by the concerned authorities. He received the gratuity amount after one year and gracefully accepted the same. He knew that he had lost a substantial amount of interest due to the callous and indifferent attitude of concerned person(s). Yet, he did not pursue the matter.

Father had the opportunity to opt for pension. But he did not opt for the same. He has his justifications for the same. If he had opted for pension, he would have been drawing a substantial amount as pension.   (This is something that I know) But he never regrets his decision. At the present moment, he has in his Bank account – remnants of compensation received on giving up the residential rights of our home in Jai Ratna Building and sale proceeds from the sale of a small   flat in Parvati Chambers. He is more than satisfied with the quarterly income that he receives. He is able to save some amount from this income as well.

Now one may be wondering what he did with the terminal benefits that he received.   At that time, he received around Rs. 5,80,000/- as PF (a substantial amount in 1991) He had invested some of the portion in quarterly income scheme. In 1996, I was planning to extend my house. I had made arrangements only for the first floor and accordingly got the construction plan approved from Municipal Corporation. But he was not comfortable with seeing my brother having two floors on his side of the house and only one floor on my side. So he offered his funds to me and forcefully persuaded me to get the extension of the house plan revised to include 2nd floor as well. He told me that when the construction work is under process, the extension can take place easily. Afterwards, it will be very difficult. I agreed and then got the plan revised so that 2nd floor of the house could also be constructed. Since I was in Bank, I did not allow prepayment of the fixed deposits. I suggested that he take a loan against FDR and that I will be repaying the loan and the interest thereon. As a result, I could build the second floor of my house.

A few years after his retirement, the Bank had inadvertently deducted tax of about Rs. 1000/- on the quarterly income that he was receiving. Since I was a member of staff (not the same branch), I told the authorities in the Bank that they have wrongly deducted tax on father's account. The concerned officer told me that tax deducted has already been remitted to Income Tax authorities and there was no way, it could be returned and advised me to ask father to get the same through refund from Tax authorities. But father had stopped filling income tax return and was not interested to start filling the same, for getting the tax refund. He then forgot about the same and let the money go. Here, I would like to mention that very few people would let go their money. As a banker, I had seen people create such a hue and cry in such situations and they had to be pacified with suggestions that the concerned officer will pay from his own pocket.

This has been one of the most distinctive characteristic of father. He has never talked about lack of funds or how he would manage his affairs.   He never indulge in discussions about lack of funds. Father used to tell us, "If you are earning one rupee, look at the person who is earning 75 paisa, do not look at the person earning 1.25 Rupee."

8. No attachment of acquisitions and accumulations.

Ever since I have known him, he has not been inclined to accumulate any stuff (which becomes irrelevant as we grow up.) We lived at Jai Ratna Building (it would be more proper to call it a modern "chawl", where the amenities were good, we had easy access to neighbourhood, without any sort of restrictions) from 1957 till 2004. At that time, he decided to give up the tenancy right and not seek a flat in lieu of the house that we were occupying. It never occurred to him that he should own a flat at the same place where we had spent more than 47 years. In 1991, our house was built in Manjalpur and so instead of craving for another house, he thought it was appropriate to shift to Manjalpur. There were many in our family & friend circle who wanted him to opt for a flat in lieu of the house in Jay Ratna Building. But he politely refused to enter into any 'benami' transaction. Those people were ready to pay the additional amount that was required to retain the right of flat. But he was firm in his decision. He was clear in his vision and always took a firm stand whenever such issues had come up in the past.

Previous to that when we were kids, he and his brother Dada had decided to sell off their property – a house, a mango orchard and a farm, since uncle had shifted to Mumbai and we were in Baroda. It was difficult for both father and uncle to pay attention to the maintenance of the belongings over there. This was in the 1970's and for a certain period of time, our aunty Aaka used to stay at Saaral and she supervised the management of the affairs. When uncle suggested that the property be sold, father not only agreed, he accepted whatever came his way, without any grumbling or any discussion in the matter.

Same has been his attitude towards other things. He has never craved for any worldly things such as scooter, motorcycle or car. In the early part of his career he used to ride a bicycle. The distance between Jai Ratna building and Faculty of Home Science is around 4 kms and he commuted to office on a bicycle for a pretty long time. Possibly the physical efforts put in those young days is keeping him in good stead in his 90s.

9. No craving for any recognition and felicitations.

This is a trait that I have been observing in him since a long time. He is opposed to being offered any recognition or rewards. On his day of retirement, only the department staff had gathered to bid him farewell. (this is what he had told us) I remember the day he came home on 31st October, 1991 after the last day at work and was feeling relieved. But he had already made plans to be at Banasthali Vidyapith, near Jaipur for a long term assignment.

Recently, my brother-in-law, Mr. Arvind Gharat who also happens to be an alumni of UAA – ICT, Mumbai (UDCT at that time), of which father is also an alumni, wanted to nominate father for Distinguised Alumus Award. He politely refused and wrote to him – I do not want to be nominated for this award.

I also came to know that, when his students came to invite him for a birthday party on his completion of 90 years, he told them, that he will come, but there should be no praises for him. No speeches. Only meeting for tea and snacks.

10. A balanced attitude toward the successes and failures of his children.

One of the most remarkable qualities that we saw in him was that he never attached the successes or failures of his children with feelings of joy or sorrow. He is truly a "Stithaprajna". He never impressed upon any of us that he was Professor and people would relate our success or failure with his standing in the society. We went through terrible failures and we had our share of successes. During failures he did felt sorry and disheartened, but never scolded us or chided us for our performances. Neither did mother indulge in any rebuke. They were gracious in accepting our situation.

My younger sister failed in 4th std and 5th std and was a repeater in the class (In the present scenario, she would not have gone through repetition of class at that level) Actually she did not have that aptitude for certain subjects at that age and as a result she suffered. But she overcame all those situations and finally went on to complete M.Com.

I had a brilliant career in academics and in sports (represented our school cricket team). But could not manage sports and studies at the same time in Twelth standard and failed. Failed to clear physics paper. Somehow I could get through the physics paper and got admission to BSc. But it was difficult for me to concentrate on studies and failed in F. Y. BSc as well. However, during that year I had the privilege of representing M S University Cricket 'A' team in the local tournaments and the University Kho–Kho team in the Inter University Kho-Kho tournament. During those tough days, I had an inclination to forget academics and concentrate on sports only. I shifted from science stream to arts stream and got admission to FY BA. As they say, there is a Power of Intention in the Universe and it takes you on the path meant for you. Immediately, in the initial days of F.Y. BA, I got an opportunity to join Bank of Baroda under sports quota as a clerk. After joining Bank, all the previous failures were undone and I went on to do BA, LLB, DLP, CAIIB - doing triple duty – working in the Bank, playing cricket, kho-kho and pursuing studies as well.

All this would not have been possible, if parents (especially father) had been harsh during failures. Their acceptance of the situation and faith in our abilities turned the tide.

The same was the case of our elder sister Mamata. She also had tough times and after completing BSc, was not inclined to pursue further studies. She applied for secretarial course in Nirmala Niketan, Mumbai where the teacher who interviewed her happened to be father's student. Talk about meaningful coincidences. She was asked, "Who is Prof. Chaulkar in Baroda?" She replied - My father. She also received an encouraging response. She secured admission for the course, which she duly completed and later went on to join Canara Bank.

11. He has always thought of other's well being and welfare.

As far as I remember, I have never seen him thinking about himself, except when he was appearing for the interview of Professor. At the first attempt, he could not clear it, but secured the promotion in the second attempt. In all other instances, his know-how, concern and efforts were directed for the benefit of others.

Firstly, let me tell, how my parents went on to keep our eldest sister Mamata with his eldest sister Tai. Tai and Bhau did not have a child. Mamata addressed Tai as "Aai" and for all the practical purposes she was her "Aai". She knew that. This happened gradually for them and there was no such thing as sacrifice for Tai. Mamata had the benefit for having being nurtured by two sets of parents – biological and foster parents. Father added one more person, Amma Phatak. He told me that most of time Mamata used to be at Amma Phatak's home. So she had the fortune of having being nurtured by three mothers. Being the eldest and staying with his eldest sister, Mamata has always been revered person at our home since childhood.   And she still maintains a lot of influence over father in social affairs. No one is able convince father as Mamata is able to do.

Secondly, he has a soft corner for his youngest daughter Minal. He still feels that she needs all the support. Recently she had to leave her job and he felt that he should start providing for her. She does have the means to take care of herself and her family, but his heart went out for her. We told him that there is no financial crises and she can and will manage her affairs. But even then he was not convinced and sent her a cheque of Rs.20000/-. Now, when one daughter was rewarded, why keep the other daughter out of the same and sent another cheque of Rs.20000/- for Mamata.

Recently, when Pandemic broke out and the Prime Minister made an appeal for donation, father was the first person amongst us to donate funds. He donated Rs.5000/- towards PM Cares and Rs.5000/- towards Chief Minister's Relief Fund

12. Preference to stay in the two room house in Jai Ratna Building.

Father and mother shifted to Jai Ratna Building in the year 1958 when Nishit was one year old. Previously, when they shifted to Baroda, they used to stay as tenants in the house owned by the father of Dr. Vilas Bidaye. It was a one room house, enough for a couple with a single child. However, father was told by his friend and colleague Prof. Warty that he could have a rented house at Jai Ratna Building. He felt it would be a good place to stay at and immediately went and paid Rs.5/- as deposit money. After a few days, the authorities at Anyonya Co-operative Bank Limited (the first co-operative bank in India) which owned Jai Ratna Building, informed him that the house has now been allotted to Shri. M. S. Sawant and he can take back his deposit amount. Father thought that since he was going to Mumbai for holidays, he will collect the same after coming back. So let that deposit amount remain with the Bank. After coming from Mumbai he was informed that another flat – 21, Jai Ratna – is vacant and he can take the possession of the same. Thus, he got possession of this pious place in the month of February, 1958 and life changed drastically for him and the effect trickled down to the next two generations.

Jai Ratna building was the place from where all the values of togetherness, co-operation and living as a community were implanted. It was a place where all the residents were extremely attached to each other. Viewing it back, from a period of 20 years, I feel, it was like living in a joint family – a very Big Joint family consisting of more than 20 nuclear families. We did have occasional differences, but whenever a need arose, most of the tenants were available for each other. I vividly recall that when father and mother went to Mumbai for any work or vacation and if me and Nishit stayed back for our camps or any other work, we were bestowed with invitations for lunch and dinner from the families on first floor – Sawant, Amlani, Falnikar, Karulkar, Kale and others. It was difficult to say no and if for some reason we were not able to go, food would sent to our house. They were so affectionate and the seeds of bonding that were sowed in those days have gone deep and today we have the 4th generation of Jai Ratna Building tenants who are still closely associated.

Staying at Jai Ratna building was a challenge in itself. In the initial period the facilities at Jai Ratna Building were considered a luxury. Mother was used to community toilets in Girgaum in Mumbai and so to have ample water in the taps and have toilets inside the house was a boon. But slowly, over a period of time the problems started creeping in. Water supply became a big problem. In the 1980s, we had to apply for a separate water connection and every morning and evening we would have take the electric motor pump on the ground and pump the water collected in the bucket below, to the overhead tank placed over the bathroom. For most the times, this activity would be done by father himself and in his absence, me or Nishit would step in. We also had a hand pump installed in the kitchen and on several occasions we would prefer drawing water through hand pump instead of going downstairs.

With all of us growing up, the 2 room apartment in Jai Ratna Building was getting cramped with our belongings.   But father never thought of University Quarters as an accommodation. He could not think of relocating to University Quarters for two reasons - firstly, mother would feel uncomfortable in the company of academic people and secondly, the cost of rent to be deducted from his salary, was too high in comparison to the rent that he paid for our Jai Ratna flat.

But today I can vouch that, after a period of 18 years, since father and mother relinquished their right to property at Jai Ratna and shifted to stay with us in Manjalpur in the year 2004, there has never been and there will never be, a more fulfilling and enriching experience of community living, than what we had during our stay at Jai Ratna building.

People not only had affectionate relations with each other, but the same feelings were extended to the relatives of the neighbours as well. We all shared a special bonding with each other, that is not visible in today's 'society' culture. We would be available for each other during the sad events like death or illness. And on festive occasions like Ganesh Utsav, Dusshera, Holi it would be a community celebrations. Attending "Arti" ceremony at the house of every neighbour who were hosting Lord Ganesh would be an invariable ritual. The Falnikar's, especially Devdatta and Niranjan would be the resource persons for chanting 'arti' and other slokas. The prominent homes where we would be attending 'arti' were Sawant, Kale, Marathe, Warty, Pagedar, Gaekwad, plus the 'arti' at the Sarvajanik Ganesh Utsav in the community hall, which was called "Lobi." The closeness that we shared with all the neighbours was tremendous and it has extended way beyond our times in Jai Ratna. Visits to the homes of erstwhile neighbours would be special occasions. Weddings and other religious rituals would be another occasion for having a get-to-gather of Jai Ratna tenants. Most of the neighbours are still attending the "Dutt Jayanti Utsav" hosted by Falnikar Family. That would be one more occasion for all of us to meet each other. Falnikar's have been hosting "Dutt Jayanti Utsav" since the year 1900 and today, it is the fourth generation of Falnikar family, which has taken up the leadership in organising this pious event in the month of December every year. Falnikar family has been extremely close knitted family and during these festivities, all the family members (including the lady members who are now married) equally come forward and share the responsibilities so that the work load is divided and the 5 day function goes off smoothly without any hurdles.

The closeness that we shared in Jai Ratna Building was so

intense that I could attend Amy's wedding in Dallas, USA in the year 2015. She happens to be daughter of Mrs. Rita Kalia, alias Rita Sawant, whom we affectionately call Annie. It was a tremendous experience, extremely joyful event. My friends, especially my colleagues in Bank of Baroda, who did not have any idea of the proximity that we shared in Jai Ratna, were amused that I had gone to America to attend wedding of a neighbour's daughter. They were not having any idea of what growing up together in Jai Ratna Building meant to us.

Our house in Jai Ratna, would always be filled with children from neighbourhood. Vineet and Amit (Nargolwala) whenever they were on vacation, would be found at our home. On getting up in the morning, instead of brushing their teeth, they would head to our home. Himagauri, Omkar, Rashmi, Deepa, Anand, Rohan used to spend more time at our place. Earlier it was Annie, Munnu, Shaila who had a comfortable and close synergy with mother. Father and mother would also take young kids with them for evening walks and on several occasions would visit Gujarat Krida Mandal, where we would be participating in the games – firstly langdi, then kabaddi and then kho-kho (age wise progression). It was tremendous, the like of which will never be witnessed in today's time.

It was during our stay in Jai Ratna that one of father's student – Bulbul Hazarika, from Assam came over to complete her thesis. The house of   Shri. Kale was vacant since Kale "Aajoba" and Kale "Kaku", as we affectionately and reverently called them, had gone to stay with their son Mr. Jayant Kale in Fatehgunj. When father requested them if they could allow his student to use their house for around 2 months so that she could complete her thesis. They immediately agreed. She had come down all the way from Assam, along with her husband and son. Father and mother helped them set the house as their home as Bulbul completed her thesis. This has been one of the rarest gesture of goodness that I have witnessed. It was extremely gracious.

Our house in Jai Ratna was a small two room apartment, which seemed to be luxurious in the year 1958, but in the 1980s and 1990s it looked extremely crammed. Mother was extremely wary of the things, but she dared not move any of the papers, books or articles of father. He had warned her, not to displace any of the things as they were important and he could trace them as and when required.

Mr. Phillips, from his department, was a frequent visitor to our house and I had heard him once remark – "I have on numerous occasions told Chaulkar Saheb, to shift to University Quarters, but he does not listen."

But this was the place where father enjoyed his stay and is still cherishing the wonderful moments over there. Father and his friends had laid down a badminton court over there with bricks as the boundary lines and every evening there used to be a badminton game amongst father, Jammu and others. Also cricket was played in the lobby and most of the batting skills were developed during those games. Father was a passionate participant in these games. However, his preferred game was the game of chess. Initially his partner used to be Raju Nargolwala and later on, Chitrasen Gaekwad, affectionately called Baba. Whenever father was absorbed in the game of chess, if we wanted any of desires to be fulfilled we would ask him during the intense moments of game and he would relent without any questioning. Minal has taken maximum advantage of his involvement in the game of chess. She would ask, "Daddy I want money to buy such and such thing" At that he would not question her and tell her, "You can take the money I have kept in the shirt pocket." He had special bonding with Jammu, Shishir Kaka, Shyam Kaka, Sudhir Savkar and many others who were junior to him.

There won't be any other Jai Ratna, any time, any where. The values and beliefs that he has displayed had a lot to do with our stay in Jai Ratna Building.

13.   Viva of students.

The viva of students – whether MSc students or Phd students, would put a lot of pressure on father, possibly as much as his students were facing. We could feel the tension brewing up in him and probably mother may have also felt the pressure at that time. This was because he was concerned – how his students are going to fare in the viva, even though he was supposed to be one of the examiners.

His anxiousness was not restricted to the students performance only, but to the well being of the external examiners as well. In those days (and even today) he avoided hotel/restaurant food and he would arrange nice delicious food cooked by mother. If the external examiner was close to him, like Prof. Achwal, he would bring him home for lunch and on other occasions someone from faculty – most probably it would be Mr. Philips or Mr. Ravi who would come and collect food.

I don't know whether his students were aware of the anxiety he faced while they were appearing for viva. He has guided thirteen Ph.d students – eight from Baroda University and five from other Universities.

14. He has been extremely revered and respected in our mother's family.

One of things that I always admired about him was the respect that he received in my mother's family, Mhatre family from the village "Thal" in Alibag. He was affectionately called "Bhau" – a short name in Marathi for "Jijaji". My mother was the eldest daughter in her family and the first one to get married in the year 1953 and as a result, it was obvious that being the eldest son-in-law and eldest brother-in-law, he was surely to be respected. Along with that he drew lot of reverence from mother's family due to his strict adherence to ethics and values. He was feared as well for his stand on certain issues. They dare not confront him with any of the issues where his stand was known.

15. Detachment from the institution where you have served

He has always maintained that one should remain detached from the institution where one has served. Before his retirement, he used to say, that once he retires he would not have any attachment with the institute. He refused extension. He felt that if he agrees to any extension, his students will be deprived of their privileges. He did take up assignments at other places after retirement – Faculty of Technology in Baroda, at Vallabh Vidyanager, Anand and at Banasthali Vidyapeeth in Rajasthan. But he strictly refused any assignment at Faculty of Home Science. And in the last more than 30 years of retirement, he has hardly visited the Faculty for 5 occasions, the last being on 19th October, 2021, when his students invited him to the Faculty to felicitate him on completing 90 years.

16. He has been a judicious person and has expressed it forcefully.

This thing came to my knowledge when I was issued a charge sheet for refusing to accompany the Bank's athletic team for the inter-zonal tournament in the year 1990. Some of us were trapped in an issue, which was not of our making. After the drama ended, I was stopped from representing the Bank's All India Cricket team and then suspended from all sports in Bank. Those were a bit tough times. My father stood by me. There were many officials in Bank who wanted me to apologize for the incident (of not accompanying the athletic team) so that the authorities in Bank could pardon me. But since I was not allowed to proceed for the Inter Bank Cricket tournament, I was slighted. Father told me – "Don't say sorry." They have already punished you by not allowing you to play in the Inter Bank Cricket Tournament. Be ready for any type of punishment, even if there is reduction in increments. (I was told that reduction of increments would be the punishment, if found guilty)

He then told me of an incident where he was the Inquiry Authority in a disciplinary proceedings in Faculty of Home Science. The charge sheeted employee had gone on unauthorised leave for which his pay was deducted. The disciplinary authority in the faculty was keen that the employee be made to suffer further loss – reduction in salary. But as an Inquiry Officer, he stated in his remarks that salary of the employee has already been deducted and he should not be subjected to any further punishment. Father never yielded to pressure tactics and seemed to be a good astute person.

45

17. He has been an extremely friendly person, sociable with all his nephews and nieces from - his side and mother's side.

This has been one of the qualities that I have found in him right from the time I could understand behaviour and relationships. He had a special bonding with Dr. Arvind Vartak, son of his sister – Aaka, affectionately called "Chotu" and for us "Bhai", who has written the 'Forward' for this book. 'Bhai' and father grew up almost together – a difference of 10 years between them and he keeps on telling me lot of incidences where Bhai was there. Bhai owned a new bicycle and he could ride it through various villages for his study and other excursions. They have been fond of the each other since then and today also, they share a special bond. They can talk on varying issues for hours together and have contrasting views.

Mandu Tai is the first person of our generation. She started addressing father as "Kaka", being the brother of her father. The name "Kaka" has remained with him since then. As a result Mamata and Nishit also started calling him Kaka. The younger siblings copy what the elder sibling is doing. As a result, father was never addressed as "Baba" or "Pappa" as a father is addressed in Marathi. Me and Minal started calling him "Daddy" since we were in America in our infanthood and the word "daddy" stuck with us.

Pushpa, his second niece is very exhilarating and always in good cheer. He always liked to play pranks with her and she likes it.

There is a long list of nephews and nieces from his side and mother's side. He loved kidding with them and having fun. It was the same way with young people in Jai Ratna. His kidding would annoy these youngsters and they would complain to mother – Kaka is troubling us. She would advise them, don't answer him. If you answer his questions he will keep on pestering you. Those were all lovely moments which left us laughing.

18. Marriages in the family

Marriage is a responsibility that every father, rather every parent, looks forward to fulfil with great passion. Father has never liked pompous weddings and felt that it is a wasteful expenditure. He preferred registered marriages. But the only marriage that was conducted as registered marriage was of our eldest sister Mamata. She fell in love with, our Jijaji Mr. Satish in a "short hand class" and their marriage was a registered one, with reception at Chotu Bhai's residence in Wadala, attended by close relatives.

Minal's marriage took quite some time, before she got married to Shishir. When the procedure for finding a groom was underway, father was extremely submissive, as we find it in Hindi movies. I personally didn't like my father's submissive attitude, but we dare not talk about this to him.

Nishit got married to Sushama, who's family was known to us.

I got married to Bhavana in the year 1994.

Today, it is more than 25 years since Minal got married (last amongst us to get married) and I am sure father must be feeling extremely satisfied seeing all the four of his children well settled in life with their own families. He loves being with his grand children and now he has company of 2 lovely great grand daughters – Eva and Sia, with whom he enjoys having pranks and playing games.

19.	The journey from being the sole wage earner in the family to being part of the family, where mother was the only non-earning person.

This aspect is something that I am proud of and it is truly a culmination of all his struggles and tough times. As far as I remember, in the early 70s, he was the sole bread earner and there were 6 dependents – we 4 siblings, mother and Tai (our 'Atya' in Mumbai, with whom Mamata used to stay). I remember he would send money to Mamata vide Money Order through post office. During those days, there was no overdraft facilities nor credit card facilities and one had to manage within the monthly income. We could sense that money was a scarce commodity and we could never indulge in any luxurious purchases. Purchasing a ceiling fan was a big event in our society in those days. People in those days, used to have a table fan and we had to manage with that facility. At night the same table fan would rotate so that it could throw wind on all those sleeping in a room.

Such conditions were prevailing in most of the households and people never felt that they were lacking any of the comforts. Fridge was not available in every household as it is today. In Jai Ratna Building, no one had a telephone connection. There were a couple of families having a two wheeler and that also, would be shared by the siblings. AC was a luxury item only seen in offices – that also in Manager's cabin.

One's earnings were spent on necessities only. And funds would be depleted by 20th of the month, when mother would start lamenting - now it is month end. In such conditions father always had a tenacity to keep things under control. We were fortunate to have a grocery shop owner – Shri. Muljibhai, (shop in Khanderao Market) who would give groceries on credit (not credit card) and the bills would remain outstanding for 3 to 4 months. Father used to pay only one third of the total outstanding and let the other amount be carried forwarded (without any interest as is done now a days in credit card bills)

When he purchased the flat in Parwati Chambers around the year 1978, he required funds around Rs.16000/-, being half the amount of cost of the flat. The other half was to be paid in instalments of Rs. 200/- pm. Here also I remember, Bhai (Dr. Arvind Vartak) had provided a portion of the funds, which were returned to him after quite a long time. He was gracious not to accept any interest on the funds that he had provided.

Soon all the tough times (as far as finance is concerned) came to an end. Sister got a job in Mumbai in the year 1979, brother in the year 1980, me in 1982 and Minal in the year 1985. So for the last 6 years of his service period, in comparison to the conditions prevailing in other households, we were quite comfortable. I could sense that people around us noticed it - seeing father in a family where everyone was earning – especially both the sons having a fairly good paying job. At that time the movie – "Avtar" was released in which Rajesh Khanna, the hero was ditched by his two sons. And I remember people telling my father – "Kaka, you ought to see the movie Avtar." Father listened to them naively. He would reply, "What is destined, will happen, why worry about it just now."

Today, life has come through a full circle and there is no one going to work to earn wages (except for Minal, who will be retiring this year). All have retired from their prime vocations and are drawing pension and/or other retirement benefits.

20. Taking care of stray animals and birds has been his and mother's hallmark.

Father and mother both came from farmer's family and were quite accustomed to having domestic animals – cows, buffaloes, cats, dogs, parrots in their household and so they both had an affinity to these creatures. Mother used to call them – "muka prani", means mute animals and feeding these creatures and caring for them, was a habit inculcated in us since our Jai Ratna days.

There used to be a black dog over there, whom we used to call "Sheru." A very lovable dog who used to sit at the doorstep of our house. He didn't bark at people and was very affectionate. He used to follow us from Jai Ratna Building to the Siddhi Vinayak Temple in Dandia Bazaar area, whenever me or Minal went for Darshan of Lord Ganesh. On quite a few occasions he had entered the temple premises also. He would return back from that far off place. Those days our mode of travel was bicycle and since the habit of "Sheru" was a bit dangerous with regard to the traffic, whenever we wanted to visit temple, we would ensure that "Sheru" is not around.

Then there were the cats in our household. There was a milk vendor in Jai Ratna Building's shopping area and he had a cat which stayed at the shop. One day, the vendor's wife passed away and the shop continued to remain closed for days together. The cat started roaming and meowing in Jai Ratna Building looking for food and milk.

When mother came to know that the cat belonged to the 'Bhaiyaji' who had lost his wife, whenever the cat came near our house, mother would serve her milk and later on milk with 'roti' crushed into it. The cat visit became a regular feature at our house. That cat gave birth to one more cat and thus started the chain of cats in our household. The second cat gave birth to 2 beautiful white male cats. They were really cute and we had named them Chintu and Pintu. When they were born, mother thought that they would be a nuisance in our household and wondered how we would take care of them. When people saw them, there were many request for their adoption. The domestic maid insisted that she be given the two little kittens. Mother relented and allowed the two little kittens to be taken away. We were feeling a bit emotional.   But mother told us that in villages they had this practice of leaving the kittens in distance places, away from the house so that the young animals find a new way of living. But the parting of the two little kittens was a catastrophic event. For 2 days the mother cat kept on meowing, crying relentlessly day and night. Then we requested the "Bai", the domestic maid to bring back those kittens back. But she told us that the kittens were taken by her acquaint who stayed in Kisan Wadi, a congested slum area, quite a distance from our place. Now this was the first time we went to Kisan Wadi, to search for the person who had taken the kittens. We were a bit sceptical – how could we locate the house of the person who had taken the kittens. Providence was shinning on us, when we found him and most significantly found the kittens. We told him that the mother cat is crying profusely and pleaded with him to give the kittens back. He agreed and so we placed them in a cloth bag and brought them back to Jai Ratna Building. It was an emotional and touching reunion of the mother cat with her kittens. I remember it was afternoon when we brought the kittens back and we could sense the joy the kittens were experiencing on their reunion with their mother. That was an extremely heavy moment for all of us. We were extremely grateful for having the kittens back at our home and felt as if we were saved from committing a sin. Till then I had never seen father shed a tear. But this time, when he came out of the bathroom, his eyes were red. Possible he had shed a tear in the privacy of the bathroom or he had managed to control his tears.

After this incident we never thought of giving away any of the kittens who grew in the vicinity of our house in Jai Ratna. There used to be one or two cats in our household at all times till the year 1994, when the last of the male cats passed away in May, 1994. The cat was found dead when we were busy with the festivities of my wedding.

The two male white cats had become favourites in our family. At night they would stay outside our house in the gallery. At 5.00 am, they would start scratching at the door, imploring us to open the door. Once they were inside, they would play in the beddings and then slowly sit near us or even on us. We used to love these two creatures. After wards, we had a few generations of cats and the cats were known as "Chaulkars" cats in Jai Ratna Building.

Along with the cats, there was one young parrot also. It came accidently, possibly trying to save itself from it's predator. Father took him under his protection and very soon he brought a cage for him. The cage was only during the night time and in the day time, whenever the cats were around. During the day time, the parrot would be released from the cage and he would fly around in the house. Possibly his wings were damaged while trying to save himself from it's predator and so he was not having that strength to fly out in the open skies. But the caring started showing signs of improvement and one fine evening when he was released from the cage, he flew into the skies never to return. There was a sense of accomplishment and satisfaction on seeing the parrot fly in the open skies. We took care of him when it was required and then when he went off, we were happy. Father has always maintained that the birds should not be imprisoned in a small cage.

The next animal which frequently visited our household was goat. The goats had that stubbornness to climb the stairs and come to the first floor and bleat. During those days, all the waste over, after the vegetables were cleaned, and chopped, used to be preserved for these mute animals – cows and goats. The goats would come on the first floor and for the cows we would walk down and serve them on the ground.

21. Appointment as Dean and the revocation of that order

It was possibly sometime in the year 1985 or 1986, when one fine morning the news of his appointment as Dean of Faculty of Home Science was there in a Gujarati daily. We were overjoyed to see father appointed as Dean. The neighbours were also happy and as was the tradition in those days, they were all asking for sweets (pendas). But before we could fetch the pendas and distribute it, his appointment was revoked. He told us that University authorities wanted a female person to be appointed as Dean and so the order was revoked.

Today, after about 37 years, I asked him what had happened and why was his appointment as Dean was cancelled. He told me that there was one lady (I would not like to name her now) who wanted to be the Dean and she led a delegation to the Vice Chancellor's office and demanded that Faculty of Home Science should have a female member as Dean, instead of Prof. Chaulkar. In a couple of days his appointment as Dean was revoked. We felt bad. But father did not show any remorse. He was his usual self and accepted the situation as it unfolded. Today he says, at that time, the staff members were expecting him to meet the Vice Chancellor and seek justice for what had happened. But he refused to do that and soon forgot the episode and went through his routine work. Even after that, there were times when he accepted the responsibilities of "Acting" Dean on numerous occasions.

22. His philosophy has been "Work is worship."

He has been extremely committed to his work. He would never avoid his duties for social cause or even in times of medical emergencies. I specifically remember when my aunty Tai was serious and admitted to hospital, he did not rush to Mumbai. He, first of all ensured that his absence from work won't affect the department and then only he proceeded to Mumbai. Similar was the case, when Dada was serious. He had some important work at that time. He completed that assignment and than he proceeded to Mumbai. This I have to mention because I have been observing contrary attitudes at work. Someone is serious, even if the person is distantly related, the employee would take advantage of the situation, dump the work and proceed on leave without bothering how his or her absence is going to affect the chain of work.

Since he was committed to work, he also ensured that we follow his way of life as far as work was concerned. In the early stages of my career, a day's play of the cricket match was called off due to water logging on the ground. As I reached home, he immediately instructed me to go and report to the Bank and work over there. He didn't like us having a paid holiday due to some unusual reasons.

23. Sixty two years of married life.

If I have to mention the uniqueness of my profile, I would write "Being a witness to 62 years of happy and contented life of my parents." Being part of family where parents have been together for such a long time invariably means that you are blessed person. We are amongst the luckiest people to have seen a long and blissful wedded life of parents.

The notable feature of their wonderful married life was the contrasting nature of both the persons. Father had firm stance on various issues, while mother was flexible, who's sole aim was to be caring, kind and always in service of her family, friends, relatives and children. Her everyday habits were a perfect synchronicity for father to go ahead with his tasks. Mother was an early riser and would be up at 5.00 am. When we woke up, we used to have tea ready for us. Such was her consistency that we don't remember her rising late from bed, except when not keeping well.

Father's family and mother's family were known to each other. My father was noticed by my mother's family and they were waiting for the right time to put in the proposal and get the wedding solemnised. Father was 21 years of age and mother was 17 years. During the early married life, father didn't talk much with mother and mother had apprehensions whether he really loved her and whether he was happy with their marriage. But slowly they started to open up with each other. Mother had told us that, when they had gone for an evening walk on the Saaral beach, he had told her that an Astrologer had predicted that he would get a chance to visit a foreign country. Now this was around the year 1953-54, before the arrival of Mamata. The prediction turned out to be true in the year 1964, when he got an opportunity to pursue Ph.D at University of Wisconsin in Madison.

Till December, 2000 it was mother who was taking care of father – his upkeep and well being. But on 25th December, 2000, I received a call from our neighbour Sunita Vahini at 2.30 am and she told me mother is not feeling well. I had to rush to Jai Ratna Building. When we reached Dr. Limaye's clinic, he told us that she has suffered a severe heart attack and we would be required to take her urgently to Shiv Critical Care Centre, in Dandia Bazaar and there she would be administered an injection costing around Rs. 2,500/-. We managed to shift her to Shiv Critical Care Centre and the injection was administered around 5.30 am. The next day, doctor informed us that she is out of danger. From that day onwards, the equations changed.

After being in the hospital for around 10 days, she came to our home in Manjalpur for recuperation. After about three months she was fine and both of them returned back to Jai Ratna. Mother started her routine work, but not with the previous intensity and all her habits – especially eating habits were closely monitored by father. He also took care of administration of medicines

– which medicine should be taken and at what time. They restricted their travels outside Baroda. She last visited Mumbai in the year 2010. On her return, we had to arrange a wheelchair and escort her from the platform at the Vadodara Railway Station to the car.

She had to undergo two more hospitalisations after that, both the times at Global Hospital, Manjalpur. One in the March 2011 and the second time in November, 2012. Both the times in ICU. In November, 2012 her condition was serious and she was in pain. Doctor told me - let the patient die peacefully. It was 6.00 pm on 11th November, and I told the doctor please give her some medicines so that her pain subsides. She was in tremendous pain and it was hurting her. The doctor didn't say anything to me at that moment. Soon he came and told me that we will get some tests on her and if the tests are adverse, we will start treatment. One of the tests revealed that her potassium was high and they shifted her to ICU for treatment. Within a day, she is out of danger. After a week, she returned home for recuperating. For about a month I slept on the bed besides her, so that when she had to answer the call of nature, I would be available to escort her. When she told me that she is now OK and that she can manage everything on her own, I started sleeping in my bedroom.

She was doing well after that and father was assisting her in all the routine work.

She survived for 30 months after that. Each day after 11th

November, 2012 was a bonus for us. On 24th April, 2015, she had complained of stomach upset in the morning. By noon, Mamata was besides her and feeding her water melon. All of a sudden, she collapsed in her arms. I had gone to Alibag the previous day and had to return back.

24. Life for father after mother's passing away.

One of the toughest times that father faced in his lifetime was the passing away of mother, his life partner for 62 years. She was having cardiac problem but was active in her work. From 2004, when both shifted to stay with us, she did not venture into kitchen to prepare food. She had been to ICU on three occasions in her lifetime and each time she came out triumphed. On 24th April, 2015, she said, she was having an upset stomach. Within a few hours, at noon time, she passed away.

The initial 2 days father coped with the situation quite well and had stated before Ajit Bhauji, our senior most brother-in-law from Pune, that "one should not feel guilty about not doing the best possible in the situation." Ajit Bhauji nodded and agreed with him. At night, I used to sleep in his room. We felt that he had a good coping mechanism.   Apparently, he had suffered the loss of his mother in his child hood and then his father when he was in his late adolescences and possibly overcoming those situations must have created a kind of resilience in him.

But after a period of 2 - 3 days, he realized the void and started becoming emotional and literally cried like a child. This happened for 2 consecutive days and we were becoming anxious. However, he soon got adjusted to the new reality. In the next 10-13 days, we performed the after-death rituals and he participated in the same without any remorse. Early in the next month, I went to give him my monthly contribution of Rs.2000/-. He refused the take the amount and became emotional again – "Now I don't require this much amount, as the major expenses were of your mother's medicines." "She is not here, I don't need that much amount and I have also told Nishit to reduce his contribution." Even though I insisted that he accept the amount, he refused and accepted only half the amount. Till today, he manages his monthly expenses in Rs.2000/- only.

Slowly he started regaining his composure and returned to normalcy and started living his routine life. He started reading and referring to the huge pile of papers, containing many research items, cuttings of newspapers and magazines. Later on, he never became emotional when talking about mother. Possibly he had that inbuilt resilience that I have mentioned earlier. One of the routines that he picked up after mother's indisposition was preparing tea and baking the toast (for breakfast) for both of them. He still continues to prepare his tea (of which I enjoy 2 cups – one in the morning and one in the evening), bakes the toast. He still washes his own clothes. Also, he indulges in all types of repair works, which I would never attempt and instead call the resource person. But father has developed this habit since his childhood and he would get involved in the same. Other activities include mundane jobs like repairing radio, repairing transformer, repairing electric water pump. Recently he was involved in the removal of the tree stump that was required to be removed so that a new plant could be planted at that place. Brother had called for a gardener to assist in the matter. But the gardener did not come and father got involved in the work and ultimately with the help of brother, the old stump of the tree was removed and new banana plant was planted over there.

One of things that I highly admire about him is his ability to bear pain, physical pain. I am in awe of his capability to bear pain. He has some problem with his knees and ankles. We have on numerous occasions suggested that we consult a orthopaedic surgeon for a diagnosis of the problem. But he refuses. He has his own combination of medicines, he applies some ointment, puts some bandages and somehow manages with the aches and pains. But never has he mentioned that he needs to consult an orthopaedic surgeon for the diagnosis of his pain. The same is the case when he has fever or cold. He insists on having his own choice of medicines. A few years back, he had fever for two days continuously and yet was reluctant to visit the doctor. Somehow my sister Minal convinced him to visit the doctor and he agreed. After a few doses, he recovered from the illness.

Here, the bond between the father and daughter is evident. It is said that a daughter has a special relationship with her father and he will never indulge in anything which will hurt her. And this is the equation that we relied on in case of need. Whenever we had to take any decision, a big decision such as how to carry out the festivities in a wedding ceremony – whether it was Nishit's, Minal's or mine, we asked Mamata to come down to Baroda and convince father why we have to do such and such things. If the same thing was suggested by me, Nishit or even mother, he would not listen. But Mamata could easily convince him why the said ritual or the said purchase was required. My elder sister has now settled down in Baroda and if she fails to visit him for more than 15 days, father will insist that we visit her, which we do.

25. Early childhood in the village "Saaral" and Alibag Taluka

He has told us on numerous occasions that when he was born, the village was infested with the epidemic of plague and the family had shifted to the farm to avoid being infected with the disease.

Regarding the early childhood, he talks about the schooling. He remembers that there was no formal school for the students of KG, UKG. There would be one or two persons, who relished teaching the students and the pupils will go to their house for learning. It was like a "Gurukul," but with a difference, that after the classes were over the pupils will come back home. The pupils will give some "produce" of their farm as "Guru Daxina" to the teachers. The currency system was in its nascent stage and barter system was prevalent in the village. Grandfather owned a farm and a mango orchard. The produce of the farm was rice, along with some pulses like "butter beans or field beans" popularly known in Marathi as 'val'

Gradually schools were established in the village till standard VII. In Alibag they had the secondary school, which also happened to be an English medium school. Our grandfather was a progressive thinker and he knew that providing appropriate education to his children was very important. I have also come to know that he had sold one piece of farm to finance the education of his children. The family had shifted to Alibag so that father, his brother (Dada) and his sister (Aaka) received proper education. When I asked him, whether his father was working in Alibag for managing the expenses. He replied 'No'. The expenses were managed from the yearly produce that was generated at the farm. His father used to visit Saaral once a fortnight on bullock cart. A distance of 12 kms was covered to and fro in a bullock cart. There was a bus service, but that was restricted to one in the morning and one in the evening. There was no banking facility, only one post office in the village. There was a village panchayat which was fully funded by the villagers. There was no air travel in those days and long distance travel was by ship.

Electricity was not available in the village Saaral and nor in the rented house in Alibag. In Alibag, they used to have 'petromax' bulbs, which were functioning on kerosene. The 'petromax' bulbs would shed good light. The school they studied in Alibag is now known as General Arunkumar Vaidya School. After his matriculation, father shifted Mumbai and stayed at his elder sister Tai's place in Dadar. During the same period, he lost his father and then his contact with his village Saaral was minimized. Very few visits have taken place after that.

26. Being witness to India's Freedom Struggle.

India is celebrating 75 years of independence. Father was 16 years of age when India got independence. Today when the whole country is engaged in "Azadi ka Amrut Mahotsav" I felt it appropriate to share what I learnt from father about India's Freedom Struggle. He is having some fascinating and contrasting views, possibly a reflection of the general public psyche at that time.

About Mahatma Gandhi, he says that Gandhiji joined the Freedom Struggle, only after he got an awakening on being thrown out of the train in South Africa. Till then he was also an overseas Indian. He agrees that it was Mahatma Gandhi who converted the fight for freedom into a Freedom Movement. The freedom struggle gathered momentum after Gandhiji's entry and it became a mass public movement, which galvanized people against the Britishers. The 'Quit India' movement began in the year 1942, which culminated in independence.

One of things that he maintains is that, if Netaji Subhashchandra Bose had not been sidelined from the Congress Party, the history of the nation would have been different. He was the President of the Indian National Congress, but did not complete his second term. It was only after that he went to Bengal and formed the Azad Hind Fauj. The second world war started and Netaji was lost for the country. He feels that his presence in the political landscape would have made a big difference.

Our grand father was also a Freedom Fighter, who had undergone a jail term. Father remembers that all the villagers would gather at a place in the Village and shout slogans against the British Government. The demonstrators would be arrested, taken to Alibag and then discharged the next day. At the age of 15-16, father had closely observed the perceptions of the people at that time, which has influenced his views.

27. Living a minimalist life

Ever since I know him I have never found him craving for any outwardly worldly thing, a luxury item or an item of status. As mentioned earlier, his mantra has been – When you earn one rupee, you should look at the person earning 75 paise and not look at the person earning 1.25 rupee. He never thought that he should own a big bungalow. There were no means also till the mid 1980s. Only when we all started earning that we could venture for a house in Manjalpur, our present abode. But during all these years I have never found father craving for clothes, shoes, champals. He has been managing his upkeep from the items he possesses since last 30 years. He doesn't like me or Nishit presenting him with any item. If the banian or lenga are required to be replaced, he would ask me to accompany him to Mangal Bazaar for purchasing those items.

In the early years of his career, his outfit would be white trousers and white shirt. This was the dress code that he adhered to. Mother used to tell us that she had a hard time to ensure the super whiteness of the clothes in those days, with no high class detergents available. Later on, after coming back from US, his attire would be dark coloured pant and full sleeved shirt, with black or brown leather shoes. This continued for a pretty long time. One fine day, he thought of changing his attire completely and shifted to bush shirt and trousers and champals instead of shoes.

Not only that, he does not have any craving for visiting any historical place or go on any holidays. He has visited various places in the country on official assignments – for viva, question paper setting, interviews, conferences and during those visits he has visited some prominent historical places.

His minimalism was evident in official matters as well. Though he had been entitled for travelling in upper class, on several occasions he has preferred travelling in second class. He would personally visit the Railway Station to book his tickets, standing in the queue for quite a few hours.

On a few occasions, I have asked him, "Did he thought of settling down in US after completing his PhD?" He maintains that it was easy for him to settle down in US. The amount that he was required to pay was not much. But the thought of breach of trust with Ford Foundation never occurred to him. He knew, what his responsibilities were, right from the beginning. Although, he recollects and cherishes the time spent in US, he has never harbored any desire to visit that country again.

28. Enduring personal weaknesses

It has been extremely fulfilling to observe father from close quarters in the last four years and put to paper all the observations and in turn, recall various incidents. This would not have been possible for me, if I had not sought voluntary retirement from Bank of Baroda. The leisure time that was available for me made me think – why not accompany father on his walks so that I could be a support for him in the unruly traffic. And after a few months I could realise and sense his vibrations. His presence can uplift the energy of the person in his vicinity. I see to it that I don't miss my evening walks with him. The morning walk was a long established habit for fetching milk.

With all the remarkable qualities, I have talked about, I would also like to mention that he is as human as anyone else. He used to lose his temper quite frequently in his younger days. We have been witness to a high voltage argument with his elder brother (when I was around 15 years). It was mother's goodness that she did not allow that row to escalate to the level of dispute and things soon became normal in the family. Since the relations were harmonious and friendly, we could see how much mutual respect the brothers had for each other. And as a result, today, we have immense affinity towards our cousins.

In my formative years and early adulthood, I also had issues with him. There were times when we never talked with each other. If I wanted to convey anything to him, it was conveyed through mother and he also utilised the same route. When I joined Bank, he was not happy. He felt that this boy is now going to abandon his studies. He displayed his annoyance on several occasions. His taunt was – "Do you feel you have touched the skies on joining the Bank." I was also not going to take it easy – I used to tell mother – He should be proud that his son has got a job in Bank of Baroda. There are several fathers who are struggling to see that their son get a decent job.

He also used to indulge in heated arguments with the front line Bank staff at University Campus Branch, if they responded indifferently to his queries. At home, in the evening I would have to listen to what had happened in the Branch. His main complain would be, that the concerned staff member was not polite. Since I would listen to these stories, I became very cautious in my interactions with the customers at my branch. Later on, a few of my friends were posted in that branch and they had told me that the staff members had to be very particular with my father. Gradually, my friends started approaching him personally when he visited the branch and harmony was established between him and the University Campus Branch.

These are just a few glimpses. But very soon he mellowed down and now there is not even a slightest bit of anger or annoyance in his being. Only love and love for everyone.

<u>Epilogue</u>

Father may not like this book on him. He is averse to compliments and accolades. Possibly, he may get annoyed with me and may be even scold me – Did you take my permission before writing anything about me. But I would like to clarify that this book is not to glorify father. His lifestyle and his thought patterns conveys a way of life, conveys a philosophy for living, which, if emulated would lead to a fulfilling and satisfying life. The readers will not only find the stories informative and interesting, but can also infer the "Internal Operating Procedures" for living a healthy and harmonious life.

<u>Similarity between father and a flower.</u>

We feel happy and delighted to see a flower bloom even when covered with sharp thorns.   They impart a feeling of freshness and purify our surroundings and uplift our life. Their fragrance influences everyone in the vicinity. A flower shares its beauty with everyone. It is not concerned with caste or creed, rich or poor. Their presence fills us with delight.

In spite of adverse circumstances, a flower blooms. A positive environment and proper nurturing accelerates the growth of the flowers, the lack of it doesn't stop the flowers from growing altogether. We know how a lotus blooms.

I have found much similarity between a flower and father. So this learning - No matter how many ups and downs are there in life, be like a flower, blooming and spreading happiness.

<u>Significance of message derived from father's life</u>

We have been passing through tough times and life has become a hell for many people across countries. Even as the pandemic was gradually waning, the war between Ukraine and Russia has pushed many countries back to a period of uncertainty. Many leaders and people in authority, have a feeling that they are permanent residents of this world, they own people and the assets available on this earth. As a result the ordinary people bear the brunt of upheaval unleashed by the ego and arrogance of people in power and authority. It seems they have no idea that their decisions affect so many poor people.

Just as I was reviewing the manuscript of this book (26.05.2022) horrible news came from America of the deadly school shooting in Texas. Nineteen children and two teachers were killed in a single classroom at Robb Elementary School in Uvalde, Texas. The officers shot the 18 year old gunman at the scene. Ten days back, on 16.05.2022, another 18 year shooter had killed 10 people and injured 3 more, almost all of them black at a New York grocery store. The law enforcement officials described it as a racially motivated hate crime.

It is very easy to condemn and criticise the 18 year olds. But the time has come to accept responsibility for their nurturing. Instead of grooming and cultivating their minds for flowers to bloom, unnecessary weeds have been allowed to grow in their minds.

Who will take responsibility for the world losing so many young people, before their blossoming? May be, we have lost a brilliant scientist, a great statesperson, a great teacher or great sportsperson in the massacre of these people.   They would have been great, but the society did not allow them to blossom. It is said, that more people have died in human conflicts like wars, terrorist attacks, personal rivalry, and riots than by diseases and natural disasters.

We have forgotten that human being is a perishable item, like a fruit or flower, with a shelf life of around 100 years. But he carries himself as if he is the permanent resident of this world and he can control and manipulate fellow human beings, more specifically the weak and oppressed. The root cause of the entire disharmony lies therein.

Albert Einstein in his book, "Out of my Later Years" has lamented: *It was his hope that his theories would be used for the betterment of mankind, and his chief sorrow was to see some of his ideas, which has led to the development of hydrogen energy and the hydrogen bomb, used not in their creative intent, but used for destruction.* Einstein went on to say that it seems that there is a bent in culture that uses the great genius of mankind for that which maims and hurt.

It is high time, we change our thinking.

We are all connected by the radiance power of the Sun and are an expression of energy. The feeling of connectedness is lacking and this is making life a nightmare, not only for us, as humans, but also for birds, animals, fishes and trees and shrubs. We are bent on destroying the earth, since we are ignoring the fact that we are just travellers on this planet and it is our responsibility to leave this place a better one than what we found.

Lot of progress has been made in the world in the last 75 years since India's independence. At the time of independence there was no electricity in villages, no proper means of transport, no secondary schools in villages, and no banking system. We have really come a long way since then.

But one thing that has changed drastically is the fact that people have forgotten to be helpful to each other. Father recollects his life in the village 'Saaral' before independence. People were so much concerned about the well being of each other. But now the same spirit is not visible. Today, people are involved in the rat's race and every one wants to have the pie before the other one takes it. Winning and seeking top rank has been the main motto (there is nothing wrong in having a burning desire to succeed) and the society, our community has made life a nightmare for the people in the lower strata. Not only that, there are many who have secured admission to medical colleges, engineering colleges and are now finding the study difficult. They are not able to cope with the pressure and some of them resort to suicides. If they are not able to cope with the syllabus of medical and engineering studies, they should be made aware that there is an alternative career available. Everyone has a role to play in the Drama orchestrated by Almighty. We need not get desperate. There is light at the end of tunnel. It is only a question of faith and knowing.

Let me explain the phenomenon through cricket. T-20 cricket has also altered the psyche of the people. [I am not against T-20 cricket. It is a fantastic sport and it has its benefits. I am just sharing what I have been observing in behaviour of people since T-20 cricket started] Now days, the youngsters want instant gratification. A match gets over in about two and half hours and it fetches enormous money for all the stake holders. This mindset has spilled over in the society, in the communities and people are not ready to slog on the field and learn how to get over a complicated situation. Actually 5 day Test Match gives you ample life lessons. How to stay on the wicket and gather runs slowly and steadily. And how to change the tactics in case of unpredictable weather. If the batting pitch deteriorates over the period of 5 days, the batsman has to play the defensive game and see that the match is saved. (I have been a batsman and so the perspective from the view of the batsman). There are tremendous lessons not only for the players, but the spectators as well.

The time has come for us to start thinking about the welfare of people in our vicinity, start being concerned about the welfare of animals, birds and aquatic life, start thinking about protecting environment.

People should remember that the educational degrees, diplomas, the acquisitions, the vocations and accumulation of wealth are a support system to assist us in our journey through this world. We are not going to take anything with us, when we leave this world. Yet people identify themselves with their acquisitions and accumulations and generate a false ego showing superiority over fellow human beings.

Our Prime Minister Shri. Narendra Modi was so gracious in answering such a related question. He was asked by Mr. Prasoon Joshi at Central Hall, Westminister, London, "How would you like to be remembered by the world?" He replied, "Does anyone know who have written 'Vedas'. If we don't know the name of such huge creator, then 'Modi' is a small thing." He further elaborated, "Modi has not been created for establishing himself in history. Nor is it his aim. And he desires that he be considered as one amongst 125 crores of people of the country. One may have got the work of teacher, other may have got the work of driver, another one may have got the work of business, still another may have got the work of farming, in a similar way he has got this work (of Prime Minister). There is nothing more than that." If our Prime Minister thinks in this manner, there is a vital message for all of us and we ought to apply it in our lives and start treating each and every person with respect, however, modest the work he or she may be doing

Our earth is in urgent need of kind, gracious and grateful people, so that there is harmony in living, not only for humans, but for all life. We have to live ethically, following the basic civic requirements of the society.

Thus, what began as a course of action to study and analyse father's thought processes and his approach to life has ended with suggestions for making our life fulfilling and purposeful, through changes in our thought processes.

Dr. Wayne Dyer has rightly said – "When you change the way you look at things, the things you look at change."

Let us all rise to the occasion and bring a change in the world. We can begin with baby steps, by being kind to ourselves, to people in our vicinity and to birds, animals and environment. Slowly the momentum will gather and it will have a snowball effect. We will soon be living in a loving, peaceful and harmonious atmosphere.

To sum up,

let me state my observations from father's life,
for a healthy, harmonious and fulfilling life

- Be kind, gracious & grateful

- Be honest & ethical

- Learn to work & live for others

- Do not shy away from moral, personal &
  professional responsibilities

- Do not harbor anger, resentment and
  irritation within you

- Do not allow differences with friends,
  relatives and colleagues to become conflicts.

And for father,

A
Century
Beacons